Feelings

A Therapeutic Coloring Book
For Grown-Ups

Yolanda Hawkins-Rodgers, Ed.D.

FCP

Full Court Press
Englewood Cliffs, New Jersey

First Edition

Copyright © 2018 by Yolanda Hawkins-Rodgers

Published in the United States of America
by Full Court Press, 601 Palisade Avenue
Englewood Cliffs, NJ 07632
fullcourtpress.com

ISBN 978-1-946989-18-5

Editing and book design by Barry Sheinkopf

Illustrations by Simi Raghavan (simiraghavan.com)

Author Photo by Janet Joyner

If I Have To Take One More Pill. . .

I Feel I'm Being Squeezed.

I Think I See Very Well.

How Long Have I Been On This Couch?

You Want To Take My Temperature At 2:00 In The *Morning?*

You Say I Have *What?*

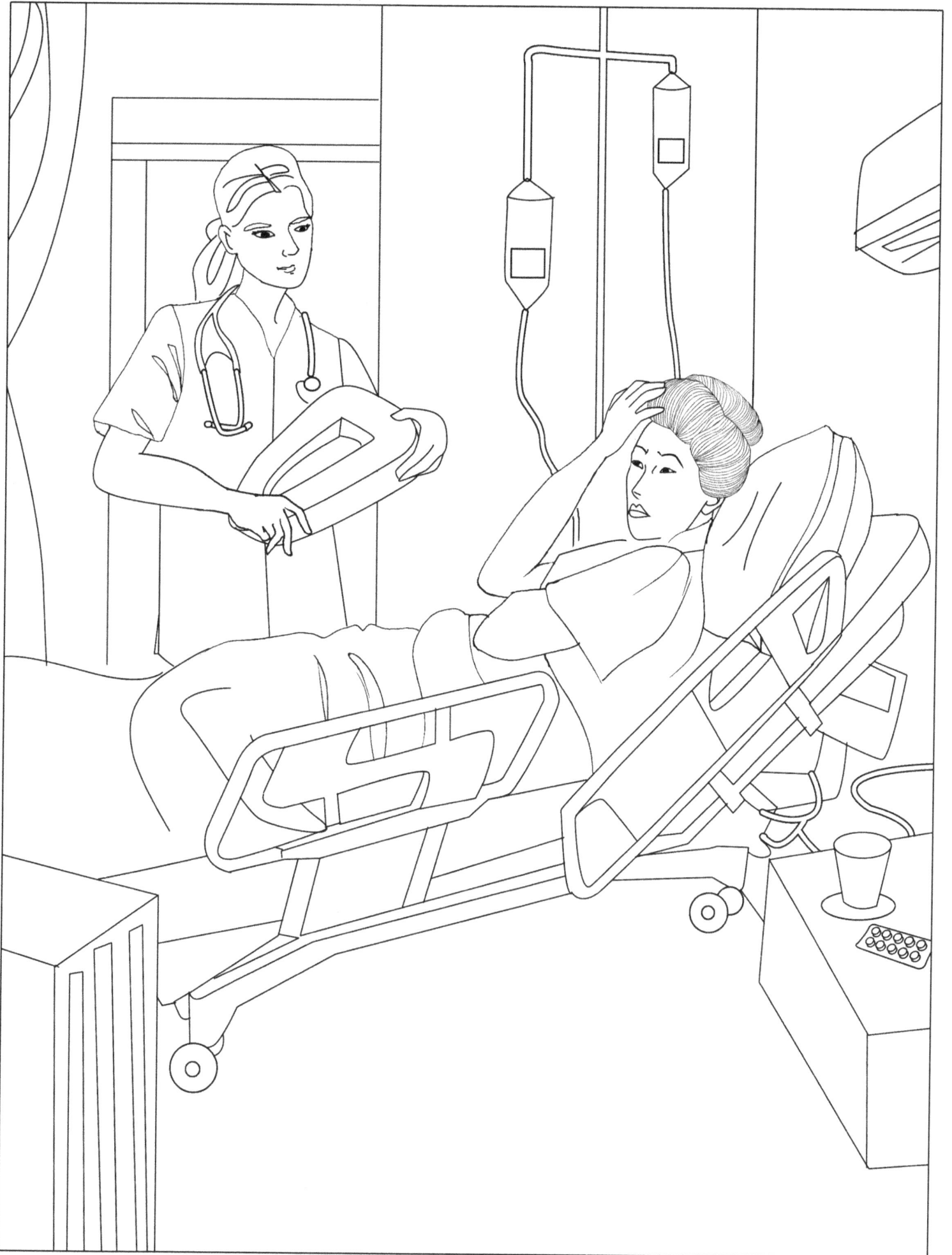

Who Designed This Bedpan, And What Were They Thinking?

Sometimes I Just Want A Hug.

I Really Do Like Surprises!

Maybe I Should Slow Down.

Hey! This *Fit* Last Year!

I Know I'll Be Back In Those Heels Very Soon.

I Only Had A *Hangnail!*

Is She Going To Snore All Night?

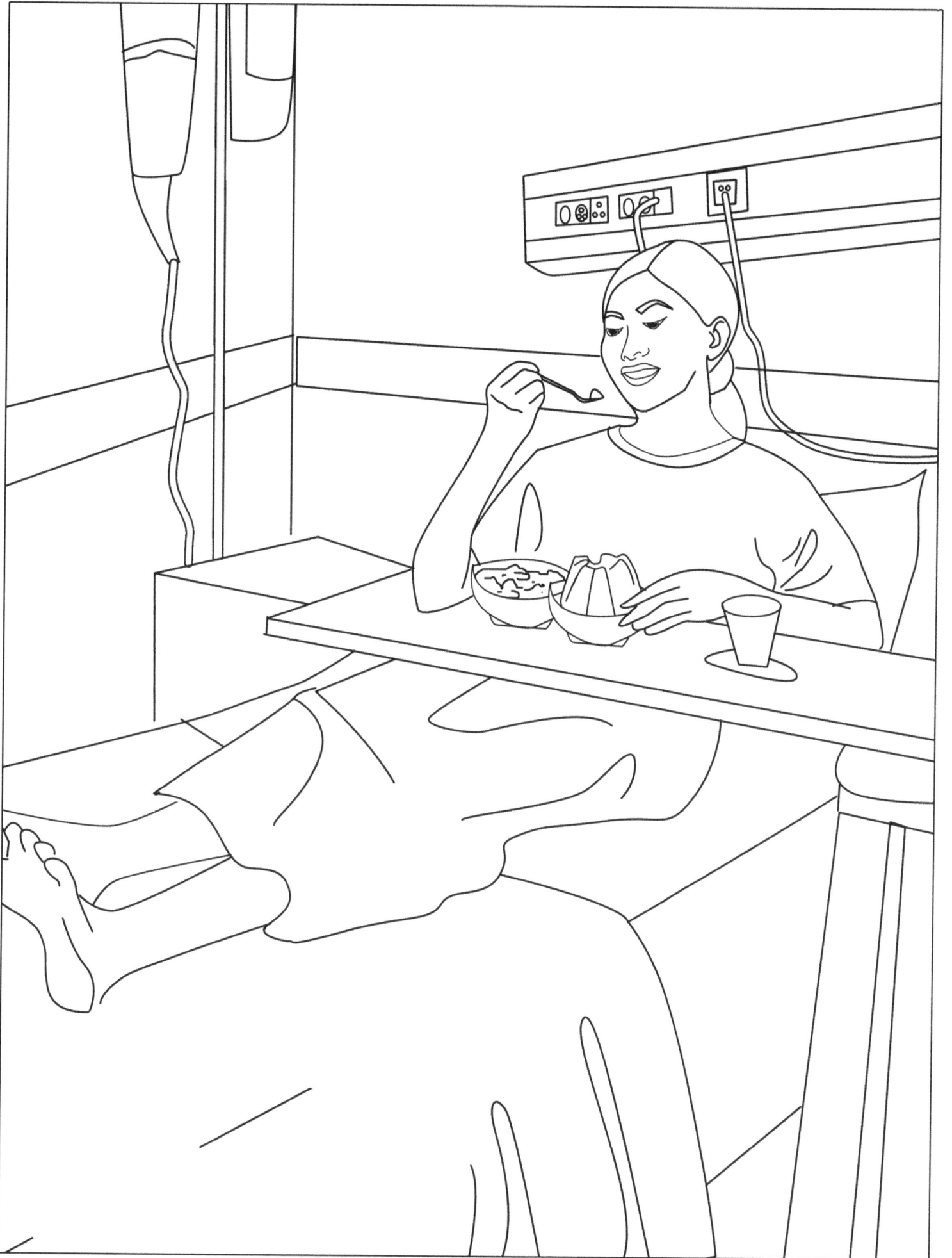

Who Said The Food Wasn't Good Here?

You Want Me To Do *What*?

Wow, This Gown Is *Drafty!*

How Long Do I Have To Stay In Rehab?

Aw! Home At Last

Please use these pages to draw and color your own picture!

www.ingramcontent.com/pod-product-compliance
Lightning Source LLC
Chambersburg PA
CBHW081639040426
42449CB00014B/3387